I0473648

I can't keep up!

Video
Status
bullying
Tweeting mashing
RSS FEEDS Video
hacking hate
forums tagging
flaming
spam
Grooming
Chatroom
Cyberbullying
netspeak
c&of sexting
anonymous abuse

Social
Networks
BLOGGING
social games
Inboxing
extremism
warez
Cams
discuss
porn
SMS
comment
vlog

A "Clear as Crystal" guide to keeping your family safe online

Charles Conway

COPYRIGHT INFORMATION

I can't keep up! A "Clear as Crystal" guide to keeping your family safe online

© 2012 Charles Conway

All rights reserved. No part of this book may be reproduced or transmitted in any form or by any means without written permission from the author.

ISBN: 978-1-4710-8726-4

This book is intended to provide background reading material on the subject only. In no event will the author, his agents, representatives or publishers accept liability for any loss or damage including without limitation, indirect or consequential loss or damage, or any loss or damage whatsoever arising out of, or in connection with, the content contained herein.

This book contains references to third party websites. These references are included for your convenience and the author, his agents, representatives or publishers will not accept liability for content, products or services obtained by you through those websites.

Thanks

To Christine, for your support, constructive criticism and love throughout. Without you, this book could never be. And yes, I love you more....

Table of Contents

Introduction

Tweeting, Inboxing, Sexting, Tagging, Mashing, Hacking, Trolling, Flaming, Blogging, Vlogging, Social Networking, Skyping, BBM, Uploading, Downloading, Proxies, P2P and Warez.

If some (or all) of those words sound like gobbledegook to you, then you're certainly not alone.

According to the 2011 OFCOM media literacy survey, 61% of parents know "less about the Internet" than their children.

It's not surprising. The Internet is developing at a startling rate and what was "cutting edge" a month ago is "old hat" today.

It's hard enough for those of us who work with the 'net every single day to keep up, let alone for busy parents who might use it only to buy the odd Christmas present on ebay or to check their bank balance.

Kids are supposed to be the experts at this stuff and the skills they're learning when they use the Internet will stand them in good stead throughout their adult lives, contributing to their independence and employment prospects, and that has to be a positive thing.

But how do we keep them safe while they learn?

Technology may have moved on, but the basics of keeping children safe haven't really changed.

If we look back at our own childhood, we can clearly see the parallels.

Our parents taught us about "stranger danger" from a young age and knew that just because somebody seemed friendly, offering sweeties or a lift home, it was no guarantee that they didn't have sinister intentions.

We came into contact with school bullies and learned about keeping ourselves safe by staying out of their way, finding safety in numbers and telling a trusted adult that we were having a hard time.

Some of us (boys especially) got our hands on pictures of naked ladies, either from other boys at school, or by finding Dad's stash of magazines on top of the wardrobe or in the shed.

We experienced peer pressure and heard highly questionable anecdotes about sex, drugs and alcohol from that kid in class who "knew about stuff", even if we didn't entirely believe all of his stories; some of us experimented with smoking and cheap booze to appear "cool" amongst our peers.

The lessons we learned all those years ago still apply today in "real life" and they're valuable lessons to pass on to our kids.

What's important to realise though is that as well as keeping themselves safe at school, in the park and when they're out with their friends, our kids have a new challenge to face, and that challenge is to keep themselves just as safe on the Internet.

As well as looking out for dodgy characters at the school gates, they need to be on the lookout for people on the 'net who might not be who they say they are.

Bullying still happens in schools and in other social situations, but it's just as likely to happen on the Internet, where the perpetrators can hide behind anonymous "screen names" and fake profiles.

Instead of looking at relatively tame "glamour shots" in magazines, our kids could be exposed to seriously hard-core pornography, and misleading information about drugs, sex and alcohol can be presented in such a professional way that it's hard to tell the difference between the websites that are there to help and the ones that are designed to influence kids into making all the wrong choices.

This book will help you to understand the technology kids are using online, to be aware of the risks they might face and to find and use the tools that are available to educate yourself and your kids about staying safe and to connect with their 'digital lives'.

It won't make you into an online expert, but it might help you level the playing field...

Charles Conway
Internet Safety Consultant
Clear as Crystal Training
www.clearascrystal.co.uk

PS: *If you're struggling with any terms used in this book, see the glossary on page 76*

Chapter 1

Understanding the Technology

> *"61% of parents know less about the Internet than their children."*
> **Ofcom Media Literacy Survey 2011**

Before we can understand the risks faced by our children online, we need to look at the devices they are using to access the Internet, and where they are able to get online.

Home Computers

The most obvious piece of equipment that springs to mind when we think about getting onto the Internet is the computer in our home. Whether it's a laptop or desktop machine, it's relatively simple to supervise 'net activity and to use freely available software to monitor what our kids are doing online.

For younger children, it's advisable to supervise all internet activity to ensure that they're not accidentally visiting a website that contains inappropriate material or allows unmoderated discussions or chat sessions. Some parental control software packages (see page 56) will allow you to limit their access to 'safe' sites which you have decided are appropriate for them to access.

> *Only 53% of parents use parental control software on their child's computer.*
>
> *Family Online Safety Institute 2011*

Older children and teenagers will require more freedom of access, for personal research, entertainment, social networking and homework assignments and the "walled garden" approach simply won't work for them. We'll explore some of the methods you can use to enable this freedom of access whilst protecting them from the worst of the 'net in chapter 7

Mobile Phones

Mobile phones are not just 'phones any more. The advent of the "smartphone" means that kids can access full websites, use webcams to chat to each other, send and receive email and socialise on websites such as Facebook and Twitter.

Even if they have no credit, users can take advantage of wifi connections at home, in libraries, fast food restaurants and coffee shops to get online.

Children will often use these devices in preference to home computers to bypass parental controls and visit sites they know that their parents or carers would not approve of.

Looking beyond the risks of inappropriate website content or unwanted contact, the inclusion of video cameras, text messaging and 'face-time' webcam features on mobile phones can enable bullying, the sending and receiving of sexually explicit photos or videos (known as "sexting") or encourage dangerous or illegal activities (such as "happy-slapping") which are filmed and shared on websites such as YouTube.

Case study:

In 2010 an 18 year old man was charged with possession of child abuse images after his 15 year old girlfriend sent a nude photograph of herself to his mobile phone. The charge was increased to creating and distributing child abuse images after it emerged that he had sent copies of the photograph to his friends (and members of the girl's family) after the relationship ended.

Blackberry Messenger (BBM)

The English riots of August 2011 are thought to have been (in part) arranged and coordinated via a private and secure chat service called Blackberry Messenger (BBM). Available on Blackberry smartphones, BBM is a "one-to-many" messaging service which is encrypted to almost military grade, making it extremely difficult for these messages to be intercepted or monitored by either law enforcement or parents.

> *40% of children use their mobile phone as their main source of internet access*
>
> GSMA Survey 2011

All of the major mobile phone network operators offer parental control features which can be applied to your child's phone and you'll find details of these controls on page 61

Games Consoles

Most modern games consoles include web browsers to allow users to access the internet and parental controls applied to your home PC will not affect these devices.

You'll need to apply controls separately if you want to restrict what websites your child can access from their X-Box, Playstation, Wii or other console.

Video game manufacturers have also been quick to take advantage of new technologies to enable gamers to compete in online tournaments and chat with other gamers via headsets using services such as "X-Box Live" or "The Playstation Network".

This social interaction can carry risks of inappropriate contact if not supervised. If your children use these networks they should be made aware of the possibility of unpleasant or inappropriate contact and know how to report or block offending users. The process will differ depending upon the game they are playing.

Some handheld consoles allow downloads of additional software (known as "apps") to enable features such as telephone calls, video chats or SMS messaging when connected to wifi networks.

Again, access to these features can be controlled by use of parental controls which are covered on page 56

PEGI Ratings

All video games released in Europe have a PEGI (Pan European Game Information) rating similar to that applied to movies, which will give you a guide as to the suitability of the game for your child.

The rating will also give you an indication of the content of the game (ie: Violence, drug references, sexual imagery etc). Some consoles allow parents to restrict access to games that are age-inappropriate for their children.

Other Devices with "Hidden" Internet Access

Some devices may allow access to the Internet as an additional feature even if you wouldn't expect them to do so.

MP3 Players, e-book readers, some television sets, Blu-Ray players and set-top boxes from some cable TV suppliers can offer internet access to varying degrees.

You may be able to restrict access to these services by using a password and the process will vary depending upon the manufacturer of the device.

Check your equipment's user guide for details.

Internet Connected Locations

Free wi-fi zones

Away from your home (and away from your supervision) there are literally thousands of free, open wi-fi networks that children can use to access the Internet. These locations include coffee shops, fast food outlets, shopping centres, supermarkets, train and bus stations, galleries, museums and other public buildings, and in many towns and cities, in "open access" zones provided by various agencies. This highlights the need for robust and effective parental control software on all of the portable devices your children use to access the Internet.

Schools and Libraries

Most, if not all, schools and libraries offer some level of internet access, which will be protected by filtering software. The effectiveness of the software used varies by local authority and in some cases children have been known to use sophisticated techniques to bypass these controls.

Friends' Homes

Just as you can't be sure that your child won't be watching inappropriate DVDs at their friends' houses, you can't be sure that the parents of those friends will attach the same importance to Internet safety that you do, and your child may have unsupervised (and unrestricted) access to the 'net when they visit.

It's hugely important that you don't just rely on parental controls to keep your children safe, and that they understand what is (and isn't) safe and appropriate behaviour online.

You'll find some useful resources to help you educate your child about keeping themselves safe in chapter 7.

Chapter 2

Internet Predators

> *"Around a quarter of the 1,000 reports we receive*
> *every month relate to online grooming"*
> **Child Exploitation and Online Protection Centre (CEOP)**

Every Parent's Worst Nightmare...

...is that their child will come into contact with someone who means to do them harm.

Children are taught from a very young age about "stranger danger". Whilst they may not know the specifics of just why, they **do** know that if they are approached by an adult who offers them a lift home, gives them sweets or presents an opportunity to go somewhere to meet cute little puppies or kittens that they should get away as quickly as possible and tell a grown up.

No matter what the story though, there's one thing that a "real world" predator can't disguise, and that is that they are an adult, and that's enough to set alarm bells ringing in the playground, at the school gates or on the way home from a friend's house.

On the Internet, it's a whole different ballgame.

Using fake profiles on social networking websites or cool sounding pseudonyms in chatrooms and on online forums, those who would contact children for their own gratification have an open charter to appear to be anyone they want to be.

To a child online, a predator can appear to be an attractive older teen, a fellow fan of a pop sensation, a peer within a sub-culture or just a friend offering a sympathetic ear to problems at school or at home.

Online predators have been known to spend days, weeks or even months making friends with a child online, gaining their confidence, sharing personal information and talking about everyday stuff such as music, films and school. They will offer an opportunity for the child to talk about problems with friends and their parents, appearing to be sensitive, attentive and affectionate.

As conversations progress and the child is more comfortable sharing personal information with their new friend, the predator may try to reduce the child's inhibitions, by slowly introducing a sexual element to their chats, talking about sexual experiences, people and celebrities they fancy, and hinting at the possibility of a romantic relationship developing.

Once they have gained the confidence of their victim, they may seek to further break down the child's inhibitions by convincing them to share sexually explicit photographs, exposing them to pornography, enticing them into taking part in webcam chats during which they are seduced into taking off their clothes or simply asking them to meet up 'offline' where abuse will often follow.

This is known as 'grooming' and is in itself a serious criminal offence even if no actual meeting with the child takes place.

It has been known for children who have refused to attend a meeting with their abuser to be blackmailed with threats of photographs being posted to their parents, or shared with their friends online to ensure their compliance.

Other predators may take a more direct approach, going for a "quick thrill" in talking dirty to a child or attempting to convince them to meet up "on camera" for explicit chat sessions which are recorded and sold to other paedophiles or posted on websites featuring child abuse images. These exchanges most often take place in anonymous chat rooms where the risks of discovery or subsequent apprehension are low.

A third of all children surveyed said they had received unwanted sexual comments online or by text message. Only 1 in 7 parents said they knew this had happened to their child

CEOP 2011

Who is Most at Risk?

Any child using the Internet could be at risk of encountering a predator. However, analysis of online grooming cases has identified specific groups who may be **more** at risk.

These groups include children who are:

- new to online activity and unfamiliar with the risks
- actively seeking attention or affection
- rebellious
- socially isolated or lonely
- curious
- confused regarding their sexual identity
- easily tricked by adults
- attracted by subcultures that the adults around them just don't "get"
- quick to form attachments to people they have only just met

Where do Predators Find Their Victims?

Paedophiles will target places where they are likely to come into contact with children, including parks, amusement arcades, beaches, hospitals, clinics, schools and playgroups.

It's no different online, and whatever websites your children frequent are likely to be visited by those who want to make contact with kids for their own gratification.

Prime "targets" include:

Chatrooms Aimed at Children and Teenagers

In November 2011 a Plymouth man was convicted of several offences after arranging to meet an undercover police officer (who he believed to be a 14 year old girl) in a hotel for sex.

After meeting her in an online chatroom, the man talked to the officer about sex, and on two occasions performed a lewd sex act on camera while she watched. He then invited her to meet him in a hotel where they would have sex.

The 33 year old man was convicted of three counts of attempting to cause a child to watch a sexual act and one of attempting to incite a child to engage in sexual activity.

Sentencing the man to 16 months in prison and placing him on the sex offender's register for 10 years, Judge Francis Gilbert said "These offences are serious and must be marked by an immediate custodial term."

Social Networking Websites

A Truro postman was convicted of 27 charges, including grooming, sexual activity with a child and inciting children to engage in sexual activity after creating 8 fake profiles on Facebook and Bebo to groom up to 1,000 victims.

The 28 year old man targeted youngsters he met on his post round, on school runs as a taxi driver, and in his role as secretary of a football club.

He dyed his hair different colours to hide his identity and pretended to be a young boy called 'James' and a teenage girl called 'Gorgeous Charlie' to meet children aged between 11 and 16.

Many victims were tricked into performing sex acts on a webcam but he convinced others to meet him in parks, on beaches and at his home, where he abused them.

Gaming Sites and "Virtual Worlds"

In 2008 Sky News reporter Jason Farrell uncovered a "paedophile's playground" in virtual world Second Life.

Second Life (SL) is a virtual 3D world where users create a digital persona (or avatar) to represent themselves in various arenas. Many major brands have "virtual offices" in SL and real money can be exchanged for "linden dollars" which can be used to buy land, buildings and other virtual products.

The reporter from Sky News discovered a SL zone called "Wonderland" where visitors were offered cybersex with avatars deliberately designed to look like girls as young as 10 in exchange for virtual currency.

Online Forums

In May 2011 the FBI issued a statement warning parents that there are an estimated 500,000 paedophiles online at any one time.

"When a young person visits an online forum for a popular teen singer or actor" said Special Agent Greg Wing, head of the Chicago Cyber Squad, "Parents can be reasonably certain that online predators will be there."

How Can Parents Keep Their Kids Safe?

It has been said that simply telling kids "don't talk to strangers online" doesn't work. The Internet is full of opportunities to connect with strangers, in chatrooms, on forums which encourage discussions of topics that interest our kids and on video game websites which encourage interaction between players. If we as parents introduce a blanket ban on our kids talking to people they don't know "in real life" then we run the risk of our kids disregarding this ban altogether, dismissing it with the rationale of "Mum and Dad just don't get the point of the 'net." We need to talk to our kids about the difference between casual interactions online (commenting on someone's status update or photo on Facebook, congratulating an opponent in an online game on a particularly good win, or debating their opinions of the latest movies or albums on a discussion board) and over-sharing information which could lead to more intimate discussions about where they live, what school they go to, their relationships, physical appearance, mobile numbers etc.

Having a clear set of rules about what can and can't be shared online can be helpful in establishing an "online code of conduct" which becomes the norm for their online activities from the very beginning.

We'll look at some of the ways you can work with your children to educate them about keeping themselves safe online in chapter 7.

Chapter 3

Cyberbullying

> *"1 in 3 11-16 year olds have experienced some level of cyberbullying and a quarter of these have been targeted more than once"* **BeatBullying report 2011**

What is Cyberbullying?

Cyberbullying is defined as *"the use of information and communication technologies to support deliberate, repeated, and hostile behavior by an individual or group, that is intended to harm others."* (Bill Belsey, founder of Bullying.org)

Examples of Cyberbullying can include:

Sending unkind, threatening or insulting messages by text message or email

The availability of cheap, pre-paid mobile phones and SIM cards in corner shops and supermarkets can enable anonymous text messaging at low cost without fear of getting caught.

Free, anonymous email services such as Yahoo, Gmail or Hotmail can also enable cyberbullying.

Posting photographs/videos of children without their consent, especially where the photograph is unflattering or has been deliberately altered

Most mobile phones have cameras built in, which can allow bullies to take videos or photographs of their victims without their knowledge, and the availability of free photo-editing software can make it very easy to alter these photographs to otherwise manipulate images, which can then be uploaded to media sharing websites anonymously.

Setting up "hate sites" specifically designed to spread rumours, share confidential information or incite other people to bully a child

Using free, anonymous website building and hosting packages it can take as little as ten minutes to build a website to provide an opportunity for bullies to post anonymous comments about their victim, display unflattering or doctored photographs and include bullying language, threats or untrue allegations about the victim.

Because these sites are often hosted outside of the UK it can be difficult to have them removed once they are discovered.

Using fake social networking profiles to befriend somebody with the intention of then "burning" them by sharing confidences

Because it's not necessary to provide identification when signing up to social networking websites, it's easy to create a completely fictional profile which can then be used to befriend a bullying victim with the intention of using information gained to later humiliate them publically. See page 25 for an example of this type of cyberbullying which had tragic consequences.

Setting up a fake social networking profile using another child's real name to post false information or to "frame" them for inappropriate online behaviour

● ● ●

Again, because anyone can set up a social networking profile on a website such as Facebook, it's common for cyberbullies to use the real name of a victim to then perpetrate further cyberbullying, leaving the impersonated child to take the blame for the behaviour.

Examples of Cyberbullying Messages

"Shut the f*** up get out of life nobody likes you go die in a f***ing hole your life is not worth living and your entire family hates you" **Twitter.com February 2012**

"I know where you live. I like the purple teddy on your bed" **Text message received by 13 year old girl December 2011**

"I f***ing hate that little bitch. I wanna bust her ass. Anyone wanna help?" **Online forum November 2011 (target: 12 years old)**

"I seriously hate that little cowbag. Look at her profile pic. Oooh, she thinks she's all that. NOT!" **AboutEveryone.com (now defunct) October 2011 (target: 10 years old)**

"They started phoning me saying that I was in the cow club and that I should phone the loser line...they got my friend's little sister to whisper stuff like 'I'm going to kill you." **Reported to a BBC researcher by a 10 year old girl**

• • •

"Three year 7 students were suspended from a Sydney private school after they posted violent images on the internet depicting a fellow classmate being murdered with a machine gun" **cyberbullying.info**

"I hate it when I wake up in the morning and [name removed] is still alive" **Facebook page February 2012**

Effects of Cyberbullying

When bullying happens at school the effects can be harmful.

Name calling, stealing or hiding property, deliberately isolating a child amongst their peers, or physical violence can all take their toll on a bullied child and at no point would anyone suggest that it's not a real problem.

> *I didn't talk to anyone at school for ages because I was looking at everyone around me thinking "was it you?"*
>
> 13 year old Cyberbullying victim

On a positive note however, when a child is bullied in the "real world", they can take steps to avoid the bullies, tell a trusted adult about the problem and hopefully get some resolution. They know who is responsible, and more importantly, who amongst their schoolmates they can rely upon for support and friendship.

Cyberbullying is different. Often, the bullies will use fake profiles, disposable email addresses, free, untraceable web hosting accounts and other online services to make sure that the victim has no idea who is perpetrating the bullying.

Social Isolation

Cyberbullying victims can feel completely isolated from their peers because they don't know who to trust any more.

When Jessie (13) started receiving emails from "The 'We All Hate You' Club" calling her fat, ugly and spotty she was devastated.

"I got about 20 emails in one weekend, all saying horrible things like "you're fat and everyone hates you", "you'll never get a boyfriend because boys don't like ugly girls" and "you're so spotty you should be in a [popular spot cream brand] advert" I was really upset. Because the emails didn't have anybody's name on them, when I showed them to my mum she didn't really know what to do. I replied to them at first, saying 'leave me alone' but I just got more nasty emails back so I stopped."

"I didn't talk to anyone at school for ages because I was looking at everyone around me thinking "was it you?"

Loss of Self-Esteem

Kids can't win. Anything that makes them stand out makes them a target for bullies. If they're clever, they're a "swot", if they're not so clever, they're "thick". If they're overweight, they're "fatty" but if they're thin then it's "stick insect". If they have rich parents they come in for stick, but if their parents are not affluent then they'll be picked on for that. The reality is that bullies don't really need a reason to bully, they just decide on a victim and then find the "excuse" to target them later.

* * *

The problem is that if a child is told long enough and hard enough that they're "thick", "fat", "ugly" and so on, they'll start to believe it.

Fear

"We're going to get you." This simple but chilling text message was sent to 15 year old Matt in December of 2010.

"I had no idea what I'd done to deserve it" said Matt. "What I did know was that I didn't want to be 'got' so I stopped going to youth club, and had to get my mum to pick me up from school every afternoon so I didn't have to walk home on my own."

Anger and Retaliation

"I got into trouble at school because I punched a boy who I thought was cyberbullying me"

That was the problem for 11 year old James after he received over 300 bullying messages on instant messaging program Windows Live Messenger.

"Somebody had sent me a friend request pretending to be a boy in my class. Then he sent me loads and loads of horrible messages every time I went online. They [the messages] carried on all the way through the school holidays, and on the first day back I didn't even talk to the boy about it. I was so angry that I punched him in the face. I found out afterwards that it wasn't him and I'd hit him for nothing. I felt really guilty about it, but it was too late then. He doesn't talk to me now and I never found out who was sending the messages."

● ● ●

Depression

By the time she was 13 years old, Missouri born Megan Meier had been under the care of doctors for 5 years. Diagnosed with Attention Deficit Disorder (ADD) and depression, and plagued by self esteem issues surrounding her weight, Megan was clearly a vulnerable child.

According to her family, Megan had difficulty relating to other children, feeling that they really didn't "get" her or understand her particular issues.

Megan turned to online social network Myspace to connect with other kids who might understand her better than her peers at school.

Soon after establishing her Myspace profile, Megan befriended 16 year old Josh Evans. They exchanged photographs, and emails but, conscious of her own safety and privacy, Megan never sought a meeting with Josh, and they never exchanged telephone numbers.

They did spend a great deal of time chatting online, sharing photographs with each other and by her own admission, Megan thought he was "cute" and hoped that a romantic relationship might be on the cards at some point in the future.

After several months of online contact, the tone of Josh's messages to Megan began to take on a different tone. One message said "I've heard that you're not very nice to your friends" and others of similar tone followed.

Messages and emails that Megan had sent to Josh started to appear on public bulletin boards around the Internet, containing personal and private information that Megan had entrusted to Josh during their friendship.

On October 15th 2006 Josh sent a message to Megan which read:

"Everybody in O'Fallon knows how you are. You are a bad person and everybody hates you. Have a shitty rest of your life. The world would be a better place without you."

Megan responded with a message reading *"You're the kind of boy a girl would kill herself over."*

20 minutes later, Megan was found hanging in her bedroom closet. Despite all attempts at resuscitation, she was pronounced dead the next day.

This sounds like a typical falling-out between teenagers that had tragic consequences. Unfortunately, it was anything but.

Earlier in 2006, just before she opened her Myspace account, Megan had a falling out with her long-time best friend Sarah.

Prior to the falling out, Megan had been invited along on family holidays with the Drews, and both Sarah and her mother were aware of both Megan's vulnerability and her prescribed medication, which included three different anti-depressants.

Sarah suspected that Megan had been saying unkind things about her on Myspace and went to her mother, 48 year old Lori Drew for advice.

Instead of doing what most parents would do, visiting Megan's mother to have a chat about the falling out and trying to resolve it, Lori Drew, along with Sarah and another girl, 18 year old Ashley Grills, set up the Josh Evans account with the intention of befriending Megan to gain access to her Myspace profile and see if anything had been written about Sarah.

Between them, Lori and Sarah Drew, along with Ashley Grills, sent messages and emails, and participated in AOL messenger chats with Megan, extracting as much information as possible from her to enable their plan to humiliate Megan as completely as possible.

There was no specific legislation at the time covering cyberbullying and as such Lori Drew was convicted of 3 counts of "accessing a computer without authorisation" in violation of Myspace terms and conditions. These convictions were subsequently set aside on appeal and no further charges were filed.
The US has now passed legislation that makes "Digital Harassment" a criminal offence and had this happened today Lori Drew could have been charged with aggravated stalking with a maximum penalty of up to 4 years imprisonment.

Tragically, Megan's story is not the only example of vulnerable teenagers driven to suicide by cyberbullies.

Natasha McBride

15 year old Natasha McBride was driven to taking her own life after hundreds of bullying comments were posted on social networking website Formspring.

Sickeningly, only hours after her death, further comments were posted on a Facebook page set up in memory of the teenager. In 2011, 25 year old Sean Duffy from Reading was jailed for eighteen weeks and banned from social networking websites for five years for "trolling" Natasha's page, and 3 other memorial pages.

Phoebe Prince

In March 2010, nine teenagers were charged with offences relating to the cyberbullying that led to the suicide of 15 year old Phoebe Prince.

Phoebe was apparently targeted by a group known as the 'Mean Girls' after she started dating a popular senior football player at her school.

Pupils said Phoebe was called 'Irish slut' and 'whore' on Twitter, Craigslist, Facebook and Formspring over a four month period leading up to her death.

These are just a few extreme examples of how cyberbullying can have a devastating effect not only on the victim, but on their families and friends.

Signs of Cyberbullying

Signs of emotional distress during or after using the Internet or the phone

When kids have 24/7 access to the Internet or their mobile phone, bullies have 24/7 access to them. If your child appears distressed or upset after using the 'net or their mobile phone, it may be a sign that someone is using this technology to harass or upset them.

Being very protective or secretive of their digital life

Whilst it's normal for teens to treat their "online life" as separate from their "real life" and thus to exclude their parents from digital activity, a child who hides their browsing history, closes down web browser windows when you walk into the room or is otherwise secretive about what's going on online may be hiding a problem.

Avoiding school, friends, and group activities

As noted earlier, the anonymous nature of cyberbullying can lead to a child becoming socially isolated because they don't know who is responsible for the bullying.

Changes in behaviour at home

It's common for children who are being bullied to take their frustration out on siblings or parents at home, simply because they can't take it out on the anonymous perpetrator of the bullying.

What to do if your child is being cyberbullied

Despite the anonymous nature of cyberbullying, there are things you can do to help your child if they're being targeted. The measures available to you differ depending upon the methods being used by the bully.

Regardless of the method however, you should:

Stay calm

Bullies thrive on eliciting a response to their behaviour. Responding to a nasty text message or email, commenting on a "hate site" or otherwise reacting to the bullying will only result in further attacks.

Never respond to cyberbullying messages at all, even to tell the bully what you think of them or to refute a spurious allegation, and encourage your child not to confront anyone that they suspect of being the bully.

Collect evidence

However hurtful the comments, save a copy of them for use as evidence should it be required. Print copies of emails, save offensive text messages and take screenshots of "hate sites" including the URL (web address) and keep a diary of all incidents, including as many details as you can. There's a useful template that you can use on page 33.

Talk to your child's school

Many incidents of cyberbullying originate at school. Your child's school should have a policy to help children deal with cyberbullying and it may be possible for ICT access logs to shed some light on who is responsible.

Mobile Phone Bullying

If your child is receiving bullying text messages or 'prank' phone calls, you can report incidents to your child's mobile phone provider. It may be possible to block the bully from calling or texting again, and to block "withheld" numbers.

Of course there's nothing stopping a determined bully from getting hold of another SIM card and continuing the bullying so you may need to do this several times. You may also wish to consider changing your child's phone number.

Email Bullying

Most free email providers (such as Hotmail, Yahoo, Gmail etc) prohibit users of their service from sending messages which are abusive, threatening or cause a nuisance. You can report any such messages by forwarding the email to the relevant service provider.

Some common ones are listed here:

Hotmail	abuse@hotmail.com
Yahoo	abuse@yahoo.com/co.uk
Gmail (or Googlemail)	Gmail-abuse@google.com

For any other provider, check www.abuse.net for details.

NEVER open attachments in bullying emails or reply to them.

Instant Messaging

If your child is being bullied via an instant messaging service such as Windows Live Messenger you can block the offending user from contacting your child and report their user ID to abuse@hotmail.com.

Online Gaming

Users of online gaming networks such as X-Box Live or The Playstation Network can block abusive users from contacting them and report the user to moderators. The process differs depending upon the platform so check your user manual for details.

Social Networks

Bullies on social networks (like Facebook, Twitter, Bebo or Google+) can be blocked and reported to the website moderators. Ensure that the report is made from your child's account to be sure that it will be acted upon, as some social networks will ignore third party reports from parents, schools or guardians.

For more information about social networking risks see page 49.

Emergency situations

If any message (however received) threatens physical violence, attacks your child on the basis of their race, religion or sexual orientation or contains content that you believe to be illegal, contact your local police station or the Child Exploitation and Online Protection Centre (CEOP) at http://ceop.police.uk

---

Collecting Evidence

Diary Template For Bullying Text Message

Your child's mobile phone number:

Sender's mobile phone number:

Date and time of message:

Do you know the name of the sender? Y/N

If yes, what is the name of the sender?

Message content:

Multimedia content? Y/N

Description of multimedia content (photographs, sound files, videos etc)

Has the sender contacted your child before? Y/N

Details of previous contact:

Incident reported to police? Y/N

Police incident number:

Incident reported to mobile provider? Y/N

Mobile provider incident number/details of report:

Collecting Evidence

Diary Template For Bullying Email

Your child's email address:

Sender's email address:

Date and time of email:

Do you know the name of the sender? Y/N

If yes, what is the name of the sender?

Has the sender contacted your child before? Y/N

Details of previous contact:

Incident reported to police? Y/N

Police incident number:

Incident reported to sender's email provider? Y/N

Email provider incident number/details of report:

Did the email include any attachments? (DO NOT OPEN)

Printout of email attached? Y/N

Note: It will aid the investigation of bullying emails if you are able to provide the full header of the message. The process of revealing the headers differs according to your email software.

Chapter 4

Inappropriate Website Content

> *"41% of parents think that content on the Internet is regulated"*
> **OFCOM media literacy report 2011**

Keeping your kids safe online is about more than helping them to avoid contact with predators and cyberbullies.

It's also about helping them to avoid coming in to contact with videos, text and imagery that could disturb or frighten them, seek to influence or shape their opinions on social issues, religion, drugs, alcohol, sex and other influences, or simply provide them with inaccurate information when they're researching assignments for school and college.

I'm often asked what the best thing is about the Internet. My answer is always the same.

"The best thing about the Internet is that anyone can be published and have a voice"

I'm then asked what the worst thing is about the Internet.

"That anyone can be published and have a voice"

In this chapter we'll look at some online content that your children may come across (either deliberately or accidentally) before exploring some examples of parental control software that can help you to restrict the types of websites that they can use at home.

Pornography

Porn is everywhere online. It's the biggest Internet industry by far with an estimated 420 million web pages featuring adult material of varying levels, ranging from boobs and bums for the masses playboy type sites, to images and videos portraying every possible activity you could imagine (and some that you couldn't).

How Your Kids Could Accidentally Find Porn Online

There's big money in adult content, with advertisers paying vast amounts to get top billing on the websites that have the highest numbers of visitors.

As such, it's common to see the operators of porn sites using 'dirty tricks' to con innocent surfers into accidentally visiting their websites. Examples of this can include:

Typo-Squatting

In 2004 an American man was fined $1.9million (£1.2million) and sentenced to 2 and a half years in prison for registering mis-spelled URLs (web addresses) featuring popular brands, movies, books and pop stars such as Disney characters, Harry Potter, Britney Spears and The Backstreet Boys to trick children into visiting porn sites.

When users accidentally entered these web addresses into their computers, they were redirected to websites featuring pornography, which netted the man between 10 and 25 cents (between 6p and 15p) per visitor.

According to the US Government the man earned $1m (£632,000) a year from this illicit activity and owned over five thousand domains at the time of his arrest.

● ● ●

Doorway Pages

Unscrupulous website owners can create web pages that appear to be about one thing, but actually contain pornography.

The technique is called "cloaking" and can mean that a perfectly innocent Internet search for a term such as "livestock" can return results which appear to feature information about farming when in fact, when you click on the result, actually contains pictures or videos of bestiality.

Search engines are getting better at spotting this type of activity, but it still happens from time to time.

Social Networks and "Like Jacking"

Using social networks such as Facebook and Twitter, porn merchants can disguise links to their websites and trick users into visiting them.

Links with titles such as "[insert teen pop sensation here] gets totally wasted and flashes her knickers" or other sensational headlines can redirect curious users to porn sites, and automatically "like" the link so that their friends are conned into visiting the site as well.

With each Facebook user having on average 150 friends, it's easy to see how these links can spread like wildfire.

Cyber-Squatting

Similar to typo-squatting, this is where pornographers register domain names that are very similar to trusted, established websites and redirect them to porn websites.

Until recently, surfers looking for information about the President of the United States typing in www.whitehouse.com may have been surprised to find hardcore porn on the site. The official website is actually www.whitehouse.gov and it's easy to see how this could lead to accidental viewing of very dodgy material.

That said, kids (especially teens) have always been curious about sex and pornography and most of the dads reading this book will, at some point, have had a girly mag stashed under their mattress.

Obviously, younger kids need to be protected from this type of website content as completely as possible, but if your 15 year old does come across "naughtynursesgetnaked.com" you can use it as an opportunity to talk about their attitudes toward sex in general, and how this type of website has nothing to do with "real life" relationships and everything to do with entertainment.

Emergency situations

If you, or your child, accidentally access website content featuring sexual imagery involving children you should IMMEDIATELY contact your local police and report the incident. If you ignore it, you run the risk of being charged with possession of illegal material which could lead to prison and/or you being placed on the sex offenders register.

Extremist Viewpoints

Website content can be a highly persuasive method of broadcasting extremist viewpoints that wouldn't otherwise be heard through mainstream channels such as radio, TV or newspapers.

Examples of such websites include:

www.godhatesfags.com

Using a combination of video and audio sermons, parodies of pop songs, blog posts and quotations from scripture this professionally designed website, operated by the Westboro Baptist Church in Kansas, preaches messages of hatred toward homosexuals, describing them as "worthy of death for their vile sex practices".

Sister sites operated by the same church include www.godhatesislam.com and www.jewskilledjesus.com

www.bpp.org.uk

The online home of the "British People's Party", this website discusses the principle behind "the 14 words" which form the basis of the organisation's manifesto.

"We must secure the existence of our people and a future for White children."

Stated policies include:

"The introduction of a compulsory policy of repatriation of all non-White immigrants and their descendants", and "The abolition of Public Order Acts and Race Laws."

www.kkk.com

This website, operated by white supremacist movement The Ku Klux Klan (also known as "The Knight's Party") extols the virtue of white supremacy in the United States.

The website promotes the political aims of the organization which include:

"To recognise that America was founded as a White nation",

"To reach and instruct students in the reclaiming of their schools" and

"To put American troops on our borders to stop the flood of illegal aliens (from non-white countries)."

There's nothing wrong with young people exploring their feelings on some of the issues featured by these websites, but these particular sites (and others of a similar nature) do nothing to present a balanced viewpoint.

All of these organisations have a vested interest in influencing young people's opinions on race, immigration, sexual orientation and religion in order to indoctrinate the next generation using colourful imagery, parodies of popular music, videos and other media to appeal directly to young people and to maximize their appeal.

If you're not comfortable with your child looking at websites that do explore these issues, you can restrict access to them using the parental control software packages that we'll look at on page 56.

Undesirable Activity

Some websites (which are generally aimed at adults) may give advice or opinion regarding drugs, alcohol, sex and/or relationships and other activities which may not be appropriate for your child's physical or emotional wellbeing.

Some examples include:

www.weedfarmer.com

With "how-to" guides explaining how to grow cannabis plants, the best way to roll a joint and how to bake "weed brownies" this website has only one purpose and that's to sell drug paraphernalia such as marijuana seeds, smoking equipment and "legal highs".

www.jezebel.com

In an article entitled "a practical guide to popping your cherry" this website offers the following advice to young women worried about losing their virginity:

Get out of town. Preferably Paris, France.

Pick an attractive, mysterious European stranger who doesn't speak a word of English and is totally inappropriate for your real life, but perfect for this occasion.

Wine and dine along the Seine, stroll across a bridge, then drag your man back to your hostel and ask him to teach you the real meaning of l'amour.

When they ask you at customs if you have anything to declare, you can proudly proclaim, "Yes, I'm open for

* * *

business!" International relations will have never been so improved.

Go Primal. Get a bunch of friends together and throw a pagan party.

Invite several eligible bachelors and wear white robes and a flower garland in your hair. After the wine has flowed freely for several hours, let The Goddess "speak from within" and choose your lover.

No man can refuse what The Goddess has decreed, am I right? Bonus points if the whole party leads the two of you in a parade to your bedroom.

Do It the Old-Fashioned Way. Get drunk, get a stranger, get down. Warning: This could be the worst sex you ever have, but that's okay because it only means it will get better. If anything goes horribly awry, like he loses his erection, or one or both of you gets a nosebleed, just take a break and try again. And this time, get on top.

www.guyism.com

"The Every Guy's Guide: How to Sext Without Getting Caught" offers tips and tricks about how to send naked photographs of yourself to other people without ending up in court.

Tips include:

"Make sure your face isn't in the picture. If you stick to close ups, the worst thing that can happen is that your name gets attached to an image. At that point you're still free to lie all your troubles away. If you give a full body shot, there's no denying it, and you can almost guarantee that it's going to end up on the internet somewhere."

and

"When in doubt, create a new email account. It takes about 45 seconds get a Gmail address, and it will help give you deniability. [...] you can swear up and down that it's not your third leg. Plus, I'm sure she'll appreciate getting it as an email instead of a text so she can see it full screen."

www.h2g2.com

"Stay Hungry – Don't eat anything and your stomach will give more attention to the incoming alcohol"

"Use a drinking straw. This way, you get more alcohol input through the mucous membrane of your mouth (this also works with a rubber teat)"

These are just two of the six simple tips on how to get drunk faster on this particular website. They are followed up by a number of tips on how to get drunk more slowly whilst still consuming large amounts of alcohol.

weebstories.tumblr.com

This website contains practical self-harm tips including:

#1- Use a Sharp Blade

Use a sharp blade like a knife or razor, the sharper the blade the less likely it will be to scar."

#2- Pull the Skin Taught

Pull the skin taught; this makes for a more stable cutting area that won't dip and turn.

#3- Don't Cut in the Same Place Twice

Don't cut in the same place twice; doing so will almost certainly leave a scar.
(Not to mention it hurts like a bitch. Not the pleasurable kind either)

www.thoughts.com

Blogger "Megster" offers up her favourite tips for fast weight loss, fasting and maintaining an anorexic lifestyle.

"If you are really craving something specific and are on the verge of a binge, go into the kitchen, prepare it, and then eat it-but do not swallow! Chew it slowly, enjoy it, and then spit it out. Immediately after that rinse your mouth with water at least three times before swallowing a sip so you do not accidentally ingest any calories."

"Buy a pair of expensive jeans at least one size too small. Try them on right before you eat. You will either not want to eat or will eat less. When you lose enough weight to fit into them properly, reward yourself by buying another pair, again one or two sizes too small."

This blog also links to another website selling (among other things) a diet pill which is "chemically altered to simulate cocaine"

Why do these websites exist?

Again, these websites are revenue driven, generating income from advertising and product sales. It's in the website operators best interests to attract as many visitors as possible and they will spend considerable sums advertising their websites to maximise exposure, even if that means attracting children and young people along the way.

Helpful Sources of Information on Difficult Issues

For every website offering age-inappropriate advice or information, there's a good one which will present a balanced view of issues which may affect you or your child.

Some of these websites are listed below:

Drugs and Alcohol

Talk to Frank - www.talktofrank.com

Talk to Frank is a website funded by the UK Government which offers information about the various drugs, drug related slang, effects of drugs on the body and mind and signposts sources of help available to parents, drug users and those who are concerned about their friends or family members' drug use.

DrinkAware - www.drinkaware.co.uk

From the website: "How can you achieve the right balance between alcohol and the different areas of your life? And what can you do to ensure alcohol doesn't have an impact on your health? You'll find all the alcohol advice, tips and information you need right here."

Sex and Relationships

Playin' It Safe - www.playinitsafe.co.uk

From the website: "Playin' It Safe has everything you need to know about sexual health and relationships, as well as lots of useful information about where to go for free and confidential advice and support on a range of issues."

Mental Health for Young People

Young Minds - www.youngminds.org.uk
From the website: YoungMinds is the UK's leading charity committed to improving the emotional wellbeing and mental health of children and young people.

Selfharm.co.uk – www.selfharm.co.uk

From the website: "[selfharm.co.uk is] a project dedicated to supporting young people impacted by self-harm, providing a safe space to talk, ask any questions and be honest about what's going on in your life."

Body Image and Eating Disorders

b-eat: beating eating disorders - www.b-eat.co.uk

From the website: Beat's aims are: To change the way everyone thinks and talks about eating disorders,to improve the way services and treatment are provided and to help anyone believe that their eating disorder can be beaten

Emergency Situations

If you believe that your child has a problem with drugs or alcohol, sexual or mental health issues or is struggling with an eating disorder you can access treatment, help and advice via your GP, or by calling NHS Direct on 0845 46 47

TV On Demand

The major TV channels in the UK all have their own online "catchup" services, such as the BBC iPlayer, the ITVPlayer, 4OD and Demand 5.

These services are available on Internet enabled televisons, some Blu-Ray players and digital TV set-top boxes, games consoles, mobile phones as well as your home computer.

They enable TV viewers to watch movies and TV shows that they might have missed, usually for up to a week after broadcast.

It's important to consider this type of online service when looking at Internet safety for your children because they can allow your child to watch content that you wouldn't normally let them see, or which would normally be broadcast after the "watershed".

According to OFCOM "Material unsuitable for children should not, in general, be broadcast before 21:00 (9pm) or after 05:30 (5.30am)"

Programmes broadcast after 9pm may include references to sex, drug or alcohol abuse, violence and bad language.

It's possible to set up a password on each of these services to stop your child from viewing inappropriate material. Guidance on doing this is available on each channel's website but you need to remember to set this up on each device that your child is likely to use to access these services.

Chapter 5

Social Networking

"the use of Web sites or other online technologies to communicate with people and share information or resources." **Dictionary.com**

There are literally hundreds of social networking websites on the Internet, allowing users to share photographs, videos, thoughts, ideas and feelings, compete in online games, chat privately or in groups and connect with their favourite brands, pop groups, movie stars and other celebrities.

For no other reason other than its sheer size (with over 800,000,000 users at the time of writing), we're going to concentrate on the largest of these websites, Facebook.

How People Communicate on Facebook

There are four main communication methods on Facebook.

Timeline or "Wall"

This is where you as the user can share information about what you're doing, thinking or feeling (known as "Status Updates") and other people can leave public messages, photographs or videos for you to see.

Depending on your privacy settings, your timeline can be open to all, restricted to friends only, visible to specific friends or groups of friends only or completely private.

Facebook Chat

The Facebook Chat facility enables you to chat privately to individuals or groups of people on your "friends list".

Private Messages

Similar to email, messages sent through this system can include file attachments, photographs and links to other websites and are only visible to you and the person you've sent the message to.

Pages and Groups

By publically "liking" a page dedicated to a business, book, film, public figure or celebrity you can exchange comments with other like-minded Facebook users on that page's wall or Timeline.

Similarly, "groups" consist of Facebook users that may not be otherwise connected but share a common interest which they can discuss within the group environment.

Is Facebook Suitable for Children?

Officially, Facebook users should be aged 13 or over. This is a requirement of US law (specifically the Children's Online Privacy and Protection Act 'COPPA') which forbids website owners from collecting personally identifiable information from children under the age of 13 without parental consent.

In reality, Facebook itself admits that there is "no straightforward way to verify age across the web" and as such, any child who can count backwards 13 years from today's date can register a Facebook account.

Parents can report an underage account to Facebook for deletion, however there's nothing stopping your child from simply re-registering straight away.

Do Children Connect With Strangers on Facebook?

In a perfect world, Facebook users would only connect with people that they know in "real life", with a friends list that consisted only of personal friends, family, co-workers and other acquaintances.

In reality, for many children, Facebook has become an online "popularity contest", where the person with the most online friends is king or queen of the playground.

An online poll conducted by SafetyWeb.com (part of Experian) revealed some astonishing results.

Parents were asked "How many Facebook friends does your child have?"

11% said they didn't know.

0% reported that their child had between 1 and 100 friends.

17% said "between 100 and 300"

36% said "between 300 and 500"

17% said "between 500 and 750"

6% said "between 750 and 1,000" and

11% said that their child had "Over 1,000" Facebook friends.

When you combine these results with the EU Kids Online survey of 2011 which says that 25% of children are in contact with people they first met online and have no connection to their family or friends, it's clear that many children on Facebook are coming into contact with strangers.

How Do Kids End Up With So Many "Friends"?

"Social Gaming"

There are hundreds and thousands of social gaming applications on Facebook.

Games like Pet Society, Farmville, CityVille, and Mafia Wars see millions of players competing for points, dominance and virtual cash on the website.

How does this encourage kids to connect with strangers?

In order to make a return on the cost of building and maintaining these games, the developers need to attract as many players as possible, who they hope will generate revenue by clicking on adverts displayed in the game window or by buying "virtual products" to use within the game.

To achieve this, they include restrictions on how far a player can progress in the game, which are then lifted once that player invites enough of their Facebook friends to play with them.

This has seen whole websites and Facebook pages set up where players can post their name and ask other people to "add" them to their friends list just to progress in the game environment.

Some of these games are clearly designed to appeal to children and young people.

We've already discussed how predators will frequent websites and online services that attract children and the risk of those children coming into contact with inappropriate adults in this way is clear.

Other ways that children amass huge amounts of Facebook friends include:

Random "Adds"

Some children will search Facebook for random people and send them friend requests just to increase their perceived "popularity" on the site.

"Like" Pages

It's common for kids to seek out like-minded individuals on "like" pages for pop singers, actors and other celebrities and add them as friends simply because they share that common interest.

Is Facebook Safe?

Ultimately it's up to each individual parent to decide if they are comfortable with their children using social networking websites like Facebook.

However, apart from the "social" aspect of Facebook, it's becoming a scaled down version of the Internet in itself.

Everything that we've looked at so far with regard to the wider Internet can be found on Facebook, including the dangers associated with online predators, cyberbullying and inappropriate content such as sexual content, hate speech, drug and alcohol related discussions and the promotion of self-harm and eating disorders as normal and desirable lifestyle choices.

The dangers are very real and children and young people need to be aware of the risks.

In 2009 17 year old Ashleigh Hall met someone who she believed to be a teenage DJ on Facebook. They chatted both on Facebook and on Instant Messaging program Windows Live Messenger before arranging to meet up one evening.

Ashleigh's online "friend" was in reality 33 year old convicted sex offender Peter Chapman, who had created a fake profile with the express intention of meeting young girls like Ashleigh for his own ends.

Chapman raped and strangled Ashleigh, dumping her body in a ditch where it was later discovered by police.

In 2010 Chapman was sentenced to life imprisonment, with a recommendation that he serve at least 35 years.

Following the trial, Chief Superintendent Andy Reddick said

"It's clear from our investigations that sexual predators are using these [social networking] sites to meet, groom and target their next victims"

Keeping Children Safe on Facebook

If your child uses Facebook they should:

NEVER add people to their friends list that they don't know in real life

Set their privacy settings to "friends only"

Avoid sharing information such as where they like to go, where they'll be at a particular time or details such as which school they attend, where they live or their mobile or landline phone number.

"Red Flags" that should alert parents to a potential problem include:

A child with more friends on Facebook than they have in "real life"

Friends on your child's list that aren't "connected" to other people in their social circle

Being "de-friended" by your child or finding that your access to their profile is restricted

For details of software packages that will help you to monitor your child's Facebook usage, see the next chapter.

Important note:

Facebook has been used as an example here only because of its market penetration at the time of writing.

The risks referred to in this chapter could just as easily be applied to any social network used by your child now or in the future.

Chapter 6

Education and Parental Controls

"One in six 8-11 year olds have unsupervised Internet access in their bedroom" **OFCOM Media Literacy Report 2011**

The best way to keep your kids safe is to educate them about the safe practices they can employ when they go about their everyday lives.

The best analogy is that of the "green cross code".

We teach our kids to find a safe place to cross the road, to look and listen for oncoming traffic and then to look both ways as they cross.

Only when we're sure that they are able to do this safely and responsibly do we let them nip to the corner shop to get a pint of milk or visit a friend's house without us going with them.

It's no different on the Internet. Our children need to understand what is (and isn't) safe and acceptable behaviour online, what risks they may face, what to do if something (or somebody) makes them uncomfortable and how to keep their personal and private information to themselves.

ZIP IT, BLOCK IT, FLAG IT

The UK Council for Child Internet Safety (UKCCIS) launched the "Click Clever, Click Safe" campaign in 2010, which breaks this down into three areas of advice.

ZIP IT:

When you're online, always keep your personal stuff private and think about what you say and do.

Remember that people online may not be who they say they are. Online friends are still strangers even if you have been talking to them for a long time.

Don't share personal information online. This includes:

- your full name
- photos
- addresses
- school information
- telephone numbers
- places you like to spend time

Make sure you have set your privacy settings to restrict access to personal information.

When you use chat rooms or instant messenger, use a nickname instead of your real name.

To stop people accessing your online accounts, always keep your passwords secret and change them regularly.

BLOCK IT:

Think about blocking people who send you nasty messages and don't open unknown links and attachments.

Always delete emails from people you don't know, and don't open attachments from people you don't know. They might be nasty or contain a virus that can stop your computer working.

If someone is mean or sends nasty messages online, block them.

FLAG IT:

If you see anything that upsets you online or if someone asks to meet you, flag it up with someone you trust.

If you are worried or unhappy about anything you see online, tell a parent or an adult you trust and they can help you. If you want to talk to someone else, you can call Childline on 0800 1111

If a friend you have made online asks to meet you in the offline world, talk to your parents or a trusted adult about it. You should never meet up with someone you have met online without an adult going with you because it is dangerous.

If someone you know is being nasty to someone online, speak to a parent or trusted adult about it.

There are loads of fantastic resources that you can use to help you talk to your kids about online safety and some of these websites are listed on page 73.

Using Parental Controls

Whilst it's important to educate children about Internet safety, the nature of the Internet is such that we also need to make sure that they're not deliberately or accidentally accessing information, imagery, videos or other content which may be unsuitable and that they're not being bullied or otherwise targeted by people who may mean them harm.

For very young children, there's no reason why they should have unsupervised access to computers or other internet enabled devices and the very best way to make sure they're not exposed to inappropriate content is to only allow them to use these devices when you are there to directly supervise them.

As your children get older however, you can't physically watch everything that they're doing.

Devices are getting smaller and more portable, and it's not practical for any parent to sit with their child during every minute that they spend using the computer.

That's not to say that parental supervision doesn't have a part to play in Internet safety.

Keeping your computer (and other Internet connected devices) in a public area of your home, where your child knows that you could walk by at any time is a great way of making sure that your child isn't visiting dodgy websites.

Parental control software can help you to keep an eye on your child's Internet activity when you can't physically supervise them.

• • •

A good package will also allow you to set restrictions on the types of website your child can visit, monitor the search terms they're using to look for information, allocate 'keyboard time' to restrict the amount of time they can spend on the computer (and at what times of the day) and even restrict access to video games that contain excessive violence or other undesirable content that may be inappropriate to your child's age.

Choosing a Parental Control Package

There are literally hundreds of free and commercial products available to help you control what your child sees when using the computer. Rather than review a particular package, we'll look at general features that you should look for in your chosen product.

"Access Point" Controls

Some broadband providers now offer tools to apply controls to all of the devices connected to your home network, including smartphones, tablet computers, laptops, desktops and other 'net connected devices.

These can be really helpful because it means that you don't have to worry about setting up different controls on all of the devices your child has access to, but because they are applied to all devices equally, it can mean that blocking access to (for example) online auctions, blogs and social networks can result in nobody being able to access these websites, including the grown-ups.

It also means that once a child takes their smartphone or laptop outside, all parental controls are deactivated and the device will be able to access everything that you've decided isn't suitable for your child.

Contact your service provider (ISP) to discuss how they can help you apply these controls to your account.

Controls on Mobile Phones

All of the major mobile phone providers allow you to apply parental controls to your child's account, but you have to ask for them to be switched on.

Depending upon the network your child uses, these controls may simply filter websites for inappropriate content, or may allow you to block specific sites such as social networks, chatrooms and other websites that allow your child to interact with strangers.

Contact your child's mobile phone network to discuss the options available.

Controls on Games Consoles

You'll need to check the instructions for each of the consoles that your child uses to find out a) if they allow Internet access and b) how to apply parental controls to the device.

Remember to check handheld consoles, mp3 players, ebook readers and other portable devices as well.

Controls on Home Computers, Netbooks & Tablets

A good parental control package will contain most (if not all) of the features listed below:

Individual Controls for Each of Your Children

Most versions of Microsoft Windows allow you to create individual accounts for each member of your family to "log in" to the computer. It's important to remember that child accounts should be "users" and not "administrators" to ensure that controls can't be deactivated by the child.

Your parental control package should recognise which of your children is "logged in" at any one time and apply the appropriate filtering for that child.

Walled Gardens

For younger children you may wish to agree on a list of "safe" websites and only allow your child to access those and no others.

Content Filtering

You shouldn't have to manually configure the software to block access to inappropriate material.

Your chosen package should allow you to block access to specific categories of website that feature (for example) drugs, violence, sex, hate speech, shopping, social networking and so on, and to alter the level of blocking imposed as your child gets older, depending on their maturity and ability to deal with difficult or sensitive material.

Ideally, the software should block everything by default and allow you to choose the categories you're comfortable allowing your child to access.

Exceptions to the Rules

You may want to allow access to a specific website that would otherwise be restricted by the software, or conversely to restrict access to a particular website that would otherwise be allowed.

For example, you may have agreed with your child that they can use one particular social networking website. Entering that website into the "allowed" list whilst blocking other social networks will enable this.

You should also be able to "blacklist" an inappropriate website that 'slips through the net'.

Safe Search Lock

Each of the major search engines (Google, Yahoo, Bing, Ask etc) has a "safe search" facility which can be activated by parents. Safe Search filters the results that your child sees when they search for a specific word or phrase to remove links to age-inappropriate content at source.

Your chosen parental control should lock this in place so that your child can't disable it.

Monitoring of Search Terms

The search terms that your child uses online can not only highlight if your child is actively looking for porn, illegal software or other undesirable stuff, but can also alert you to issues which may be affecting them.

For example, repeated searches by a 10 year old girl for "diet sites", "weight loss tips" or similar terms can present an opportunity to spark a discussion about body image and healthy eating.

Internet Activity Report

You should be able to view a full report of your child's Internet activity, including the websites they've visited and the length of time they spent on each site.

Time Based Restrictions

You might want to restrict your child to using the computer for a set number of hours each day or week, to ensure that they can't use the Internet after bedtime or reduce arguments by allocating "keyboard time" for each child in your family.

Time based restrictions will prevent your child from logging on to the computer outside of the times you have specified, and will automatically log them off when their time is up.

You should also be able to override these controls on a "one-off" basis, for example if a child has homework to complete but is running out of time.

Social Monitoring

If you've decided to allow your child to access social networking websites, the software should highlight new accounts set up by your child and specifically alert you if your child has lied about their age to open that account.

It should also tell you your child's username so you can monitor your child's activity on that website.

● ● ●

Most parental control packages are unable to monitor what your child does once they've logged in to a membership site like Facebook. You'll need a separate piece of software to do that, which we'll explore later in the chapter.

Instant Messaging Monitoring

Many kids don't use Instant Messaging (IM) software any more, preferring instead the integrated "Facebook Chat" facility.

If your child still uses AOL Chat or Windows Live Messenger you should look for a parental control package that monitors friend requests and messages received via these services.

Privacy Protection

Your chosen package should alert you if your child shares personal information such as their home address, landline or mobile telephone number, what school they attend or other information which could be used to locate them in "real life".

Email or SMS Alerts

Ideally, your software will send you an email (or a text message to your mobile phone) in the event that your child attempts to visit a blocked website, searches for a "red-flagged" phrase, shares personally identifiable information or lies about their age to join a social network.

Ease of Use

This may seem like a long list of features to look out for, but most parental control packages will have most of them.

Ease of use is likely to be the deciding factor for most parents.

The last thing that you want is a piece of software that's so complicated that you have to get your kids to explain to you how it works!

Before you decide on a particular package, check out online demos, download and test a free trial or read reviews from other users to help you decide on the one that's right for you.

Monitoring Facebook

Most parental control software won't allow you to see what's going on once your child is logged into Facebook.

You can become your child's Facebook friend and see what's happening publically, for example on your child's Timeline, but that won't help you to see other indicators that might mean that your child is being Cyberbullied, bullying someone else, sharing inappropriate website links or connecting with complete strangers.

To get a better insight into your child's Facebook world you'll have to do one of three things.

Convince your child to give you their Facebook password so you can log in and check their messages, uploaded photographs, friends profiles and other "private" areas of the site

If your child is happy for you to have their Facebook password and randomly check up on their activity, then all is well and this works well for many parents. Some children may not want this, considering Facebook to be their "private space" and resenting you for even asking.

● ● ●

Covertly obtain their password by "shoulder surfing" or using spyware to log their keystrokes

Using covert techniques to obtain your child's password could lead to a breakdown in trust between you and your child if they find out, which could in turn lead to them creating secret Facebook profiles which you have no way of keeping an eye on.

Use a third party Facebook monitoring software package that will alert you if something is amiss.

If your child doesn't want you to have their Facebook password, or you're not comfortable poking around in their "private" space, this is probably the best option for you.

There are a number of commercial Facebook Parental Control packages available online, costing from as little as £15.00 a year (at the time of writing) for a package that will monitor up to five accounts.

Common features include:

Cyberbullying Alerts

By monitoring posts on your child's Timeline, comments and tags on status updates and photographs, and private messages, the software can alert you if inappropriate language is being used by, or toward, your child which may indicate that they are either perpetrating, or falling victim to, Cyberbullying.

Stranger Alerts

Under normal circumstances, the people who appear on your child's friends list will be connected to other people that your child knows and is friends with on Facebook.

● ● ●

The software will scan your child's friends list, and alert you to anyone who is "socially isolated" from your child's other friends, flagging any such people as a potential cause for concern.

Age Alerts

By analysing the language and grammar used by your child's Facebook friends, the software will flag up anyone who may actually be older than they claim to be.

You can also set the software to alert you to anyone over a certain age who is friends with your child.

Privacy Protection

You will be alerted instantly if your child posts details of their home address, telephone number, what school they attend or other personally identifiable information anywhere on Facebook.

Link Scanning

The software will automatically scan links to websites posted on your child's Timeline or sent to them by private message for inappropriate content or scams which could lead to your child's Facebook account being hacked.

Benefits of Facebook Monitoring Software

Using this type of software can be more effective than having your child's password or "friending" them on the site because it monitors your child's account 24 hours a day, seven days a week, alerting you instantly by email or text message when it detects a problem.

It's also more attractive to your child, because it lets them have their privacy when using Facebook normally, safe in the knowledge that you'll only get involved if something is flagged by the system as a potential problem.

Because the software is linked to your child's Facebook account (and not to a particular device accessing it) you will be alerted of potential problems regardless of how or where your child is using Facebook.

If they're using their mobile phone, a tablet computer, a public machine in a cybercafé or a friend's PC, they'll still be protected.

Using this type of software also means that you don't have to be friends with your child on Facebook. In fact, you don't even need to be a Facebook user to take advantage of it's features.

Things to be aware of

Photographs

Not all of the available packages (at the time of writing) are able to scan content in photographs uploaded to Facebook by your child or posted to your child's Timeline. If you are particularly concerned about this type of content you should check that your chosen package includes this feature.

Disclosure and Limitations

Your children will be made aware that their accounts are being monitored by a third party service.

They will also be able to disable the service by revoking the application's permissions in their privacy settings, although you will be alerted by email or text message if this happens.

That's why it's important that you discuss your decision to use this type of software with your child, so they understand that you're using it to give them the best possible balance between privacy and protection.

Chapter 7

And Finally...

Keeping children safe on the Internet is a challenge and as parents we're facing a never ending battle between trusting our kids and exercising our protective instincts, respecting their privacy and keeping a watchful eye over what they're really doing and who they're talking to.

We have to accept that we don't have absolute control over who they're spending time with in the "real world", the conversations they're having and the language they use in the company of their friends. All we can do is to help them develop their own set of values and hope that they live by them once they're out of our sight.

Similarly, we can't exercise total control over their digital lives. If we try, then we risk losing ALL control because they'll always be one step ahead of us in the use (and abuse) of technology and will hide their tracks well if they feel they need to.

We can't stop our kids from seeing porn, coming across hate speech or finding out about drugs, sex and alcohol from friends, movies, magazines or other sources, but hopefully we can limit their exposure to that material until they're emotionally ready to handle it.

By working with our children, we can help them to understand the risks they may face when they use the

• • •

Internet, agree with them the limits and boundaries of what is and isn't acceptable behaviour and help them navigate the minefields of online life, to avoid the hunting grounds of online predators and to understand the risks inherent in making friends online.

By being open and approachable about these risks, we can ensure that our children feel confident in talking to us about their online experiences and will let us know if something happens that makes them uncomfortable.

By keeping a semi-distant watching brief, we can also be there to be aware if they're straying off the path and identify potential issues before they become real problems.

Other Useful Resources

We've covered a lot of information about the online risks your kids might face when they use the 'net, and some of the methods you can use to reduce those risks. What we haven't really looked at here is the different ways you can talk to your child about keeping themselves safe.

There are a couple of reasons for that. The first is that I have no wish to tell you how to talk to your kids. That's not my place.

The second is that every child is different. What may work for one child might be totally inappropriate for another.

So what I've decided to do is to point you in the direction of a number of different resources for kids of various ages that you can check out before deciding which ones are most suitable for your family.

• • •

For 5-7 Year Olds

Hector's World

www.thinkuknow.co.uk/5_7/hectorsworld/

A series of 6 cartoons featuring Hector the dolphin and his friends, this website from CEOP helps young children understand about the basics of using computers and the Internet safely

For 7-11 Year Olds

CBBC Stay Safe

www.bbc.co.uk/cbbc/topics/stay-safe

Using popular kids TV characters this website from the BBC helps kids to understand issues such as Internet privacy, Cyberbullying, Downloading and finding accurate information online

The Cybercafé

http://thinkuknow.co.uk/8_10/cybercafe/

Kids can visit the Cybercafe to help Griff and his friends stay safe while using email, chat areas, mobiles and other new technologies!

For 11-16 Year Olds

Think U Know?

http://thinkuknow.co.uk/11_16/

A series of thought provoking articles and videos covering topics such as Sexting, Cyberbullying, Grooming, Social Networking, Chatrooms, Hacking and Viruses to help you to talk to your kids about respecting themselves and keeping themselves safe.

For Victims of Cyberbullying

Cybermentors

www.cybermentors.org.uk

Cybermentors is a social network specifically for kids who are having a hard time online. Run by anti-bullying charity BeatBullying, the site is moderated by peer mentors who have experienced bullying in different forms and have been specifically trained to help other young people get the support that they need.

For Parents

Think U Know for Parents

www.thinkuknow.co.uk/parents/

This website operated by CEOP will provide more background reading on the risks your child may face when they use the Internet and how you can talk to them about those risks.

The Child Exploitation and Online Protection Centre (CEOP)

www.ceop.police.uk/Ceop-Report/

This website is for parents (or children) to report anyone who has behaved inappropriately with your child via social networking, in a chatroom, via email or anywhere else online..

PLEASE REMEMBER: If you believe that your child is in imminent danger of abuse call 999 straight away.

Appendices

(i)   Glossary of Terms

Android

An operating system used on Smartphones and Tablet computers

Applications

Programs which run on a smartphone, tablet or home computer.

Also referred to as "Apps"

Blog

An online diary or journal

Also referred to as "Web-Log"

Browsing

Visiting websites on the Internet.

Also referred to as "Surfing"

Chatroom

A website where users can chat to each other either in public or via private message

Cookies

Small text files stored on your computer which tell the website if you've visited before, what your user name is, if you've put an item in your "shopping basket" etc.

Downloading

Saving something to your computer from the Internet. This can include pictures, videos, music, games or other software.

Flaming

Writing comments on a discussion forum, social network or blog with the intention of starting an argument or offending somebody.

History

A log of all websites visited from a particular computer

Network

More than one computer sharing an Internet connection or storage device such as a hard drive or file server

Operating System

The software that allows you to use your computer. Examples include Windows, Linux, MacOS and Android.

Search Engine

A website that helps you to find websites based on your search terms. Examples include Google, Yahoo and Bing.

Status Update

An entry on a social network Timeline or Wall updating friends about what you're doing, thinking or feeling

● ● ●

Skype

A computer program which allows users to chat to each other using a headset, by exchanging text messages or via a webcam

SMS (Short Message Service)

Another term for text messaging on mobile phones

Social Network

Any website that allows users to interact with each other and share information or media through a network of contacts or "friends". Examples include Google+, Facebook and Bebo.

Spam

Unsolicited advertising (usually received via email)

Tablet

A hand-held computer (usually with a touchscreen)

Tagging

Marking a photograph posted online to identify the people featured in it

Trolling

Writing deliberately offensive or argumentative comments on websites with the intention of causing upset

Tweet

Any comment made on Twitter

Twitter

A website which allows users to send short messages to their followers, known as "Tweets"

Uploading

Sending information from your computer to the Internet. For example, when you post a picture to Facebook, it has to be "uploaded" to the website.

URL

Text that identifies a particular website on the Internet.

Examples include www.google.com or www.facebook.com. Also known as a web address or domain name

Vlog

A contraction of **Video Log,** a Vlog is an online video diary.

Web Browser

Software on your computer that allows you to access the Internet. Examples include Internet Explorer, Firefox, Chrome and Safari.

Webcam

A small camera attached to a computer which allows someone to see you whilst you're talking on the Internet

(ii)   NetSpeak

"The jargon, abbreviations, and emoticons typically used by frequent internet users" **Dictionary.com**

10 online slang terms every parent should know

ASL (or A/S/L)

Age/Sex/Location

Used in chatrooms as an introduction.

A typical response would be "18/F/UK" (18 year old female in the UK)

BF / GF

BoyFriend of GirlFriend

C2C

Cam **2** Cam

To have an online video chat using webcams

Cyber/Cybersex

An online conversation of a sexual nature

PIR/POS/P911

Parents In Room / Parents Over Shoulder

A warning to online friends that you might see their comments

Pr0n

A deliberate mis-spelling of "Porn" to try and deceive Internet filters

TDTM

Talk Dirty To Me

An invitation to have "Cybersex"

Warez

A slang term for illegal downloads of movies, music or software

WTF?

What The F*ck?

An expression of disbelief or surprise

(iii)   About the Author

Charles Conway is an Internet safety consultant with Clear as Crystal Training based in Wrexham, and an associate member of the UK Council for Child Internet Safety (UKCCIS).

Working with local authorities, National charities, schools, community groups and independent fostering agencies around the UK, Charles has helped many parents, carers, teachers and social workers to "bridge the gap" between what they know about the Internet and related technologies, and what the children in their care know.

Charles is also the editor of an online safety website called Scam Detectives (www.scam-detectives.co.uk) which aims to educate Internet users about online scams and ripoffs.

Scam Detectives has twice been shortlisted for the prestigious Nominet Internet Award for "Making the Internet Safer" alongside such organisations as the BBC, E-Crime Wales, BeatBullying and The Vodafone Parents Guide.

Getting in Touch

If you'd like to discuss any aspect of Charles' work, have any questions about anything you've read in this book or would like him to speak at an event, you can email him at **charles@clearascrystal.co.uk** or visit his website at **www.clearascrystal.co.uk**

www.ingramcontent.com/pod-product-compliance
Lightning Source LLC
Chambersburg PA
CBHW071607170526
45166CB00003B/1025